Fairway to Kitchen

A collection of recipes and golf tips for every golfer, whether you play from the Blue Tees or the Red Tees.

by, Christi Blauwkamp
(former LPGA member)

2nd Printing May, 1999

Copyright: 1998 by ClassicGolf

ISBN 0-9665045-1-8

Library of Congress Catalog Card Number: 98-96604

PUBLISHED BY:

**ClassicGolf
PO Box 2829
Orangeburg, S.C. 29116**

TABLE OF CONTENTS

APPETIZERS & MISCELLANEOUS

BREAD, ROLLS, & MUFFINS

BREAD, ROLLS, & MUFFINS (CONTINUED)

COOKIES, PIES, & DESSERTS

COOKIES, PIES, & DESSERTS (CONTINUED)

MAIN DISHES

MAIN DISHES (CONTINUED)

SOUPS, SALADS, & SAUCES

THE 19TH HOLE

JUNIOR GOLF

TABLE OF CONTENTS - GOLF TIPS

Appetizers

&

Miscellaneous

"QUALIFYING ROUND" ARTICHOKE SPREAD

1 can (soup size) unmarinated artichoke hearts – bite size
1 c. mayonnaise
1 c. Parmesan cheese

Mix mayonnaise and cheese. Arrange artichoke hearts in bottom of 9 x 13 pan. Pour mayonnaise mix over artichokes. Bake at 350 degrees for 15 minutes until browned on top. Serve with crackers.

**This is one of my favorites from a friend in California.

"HAPPY HOUR" CHEESE

1 lb. Velveeta cheese
5 3/4 oz. jar horse radish
5 dashes Tabasco sauce
9 tbsp. mayonnaise

Melt cheese in double boiler. Add remaining ingredients and mix until smooth. Place in desired container and cool. Serve with crackers or chips.

"CHAMPIONS" AMARETTO SAUCE

1 pkg. (6oz) cream cheese – softened
1/2 c. plain yogurt
1/3 c. Amaretto
3 tbsp. sugar
1/8 tsp. cinnamon
1 tbsp. orange juice
6 small fresh peaches, or apples

Beat together cream cheese, yogurt, Amaretto and 2 tablespoons sugar until well blended. Cover and refrigerate overnight. Peel and pit peaches; slice thin. Just before serving mix 1-tablespoon sugar, cinnamon and orange juice. Toss with cut peaches and refrigerate. Spoon Amaretto sauce over fruit in individual dishes.

QUICK AND EASY - VEGETABLE DIP

1 c. mayonnaise
1 tsp. onion powder
1 tsp. garlic powder
1 tsp. curry powder
1 tsp. horseradish
1 tbsp. vinegar

Mix ingredients together and chill before serving.

"GOLF BALLS" (MEAT BALLS)

2 lb. lean ground beef
2 eggs
1/4 c. milk
3 tbsp. catsup
1 tbsp. mustard
dash soy sauce
dash lemon juice
3 slices dry bread crumbs
1 small onion – chopped
salt & pepper
1 can beef gravy

Mix and roll into balls. Put in baking dish or casserole.
Pour gravy over top, cover and bake at 375 degrees
for 1 hour.

Determining Your Stance:
- To determine your stance, begin walking at your
  normal pace; stop in mid-stride and pivot on both
  feet. This should be a comfortable stance for you to
  use with your middle to long irons.

"CHRISTI'S" GRANOLA

3/4 c. honey
1/2 c. oil
1 tsp. vanilla
1/2 tsp. salt
1/2 c. sesame seeds
1 c. wheat germ (I like honey wheat)
1 1/2 c. unsweetened coconut – grated
7 c. rolled oats
3/4 c. walnuts, or almonds – chopped
3/4 c. raisins

In Dutch oven heat the first 3 ingredients until thin. Turn off heat and stir in remaining ingredients in order, except for raisins. Stir well so that the honey mixture coats all ingredients. Place Dutch oven in 350 degree oven. Granola will begin to toast in about 15 minutes. After 15 minutes, begin to stir every 10 minutes until toasted lightly or to your own taste. Take granola out of oven and spread out on pieces of wax paper to cool. Add raisins before placing in containers.

"YELLOW BALL" CURRIED POTATOES

1 lb. red potatoes, halved and unpeeled
1 small onion – sliced
1 garlic clove – minced
1/4 – 1/2 tsp. curry powder
2 tbsp. margarine
1 tsp. parsley
1 tsp. lemon juice
1/4 tsp. salt
dash pepper

In medium covered saucepan, cook unpeeled potatoes and sliced onion in boiling, lightly salted water until potatoes are just tender. Drain. In small saucepan cook garlic, curry powder, and margarine about 1 minute. Stir in parsley, lemon juice, salt and pepper. Add butter mixture to potatoes and onions; toss gently to mix. Heat on low for 3 - 5 minutes, gently stirring.

- The Fairway Bunker Shot: In the fairway bunker it is very important to get solid footing so as not to lose your balance.
- Position the ball in the middle of your stance, and hit the ball before you hit the sand.

SHRIMP DIP

1 3/4 c. cooked shrimp cut into small pieces
1 lb. cream cheese
1/2 pt. sour cream
2/3 tsp. curry powder
2 tbsp. chopped onion

Mix cream cheese and sour cream until smooth. Add onion, curry and blend well. Fold in cooked shrimp. Refrigerate several hours before serving.

"DIMPLE" CHEESE BALL

8 oz. cream cheese
8 oz. sharp cheese
2 Tbsp. Worcestershire sauce
1 tsp. lemon juice
dash salt, and hot sauce
mixed nuts - chopped

Blend cheese and cream cheese. Add remaining ingredients and mix well. Mold into desired shape and roll in chopped nuts. Chill 8 hours.

SPICY POTATO "WEDGES"

4-5 large baking potatoes, cut into thin wedges
1/2 tsp. each of the following:
-ground red pepper
-black pepper
-onion powder
-garlic powder
4 tsp. vegetable oil

Using nonstick cooking spray, arrange wedges on cooking sheet and sprinkle with oil. Bake at 425 degrees for 10 minutes on each side until golden brown. Place cooked potato wedges in mixing bowl, sprinkle and mix with spice mixture.

*Good as an appetizer or with main meal.

- **The Wedge Shot:** The swing between the chip shot and full swing.
- Slightly open and narrow your stance.
- Transfer your weight but keep your movement to a minimum.
- And I recommend never swinging more than 85% on this shot.

BEER BARBEQUE SAUCE

1 c. beer
1/2 tsp. salt
1/3 c. vinegar
1/8 c. honey
1 c. catsup
1/3 c. firmly packed brown sugar
3 Tbsp. Worcestershire sauce
3/4 tsp. mustard
3/4 paprika
1 small onion, sliced
1 tsp. lemon juice

Combine all ingredients except lemon juice and bring to a boil. Reduce heat and simmer for 5 - 7 minutes. Add lemon juice. Bottle and refrigerate. Should use within 30 days.

CHEESE BALL II

8 oz. pkg. cream cheese
1/2 small can parmesan grated cheese
1 pkg. garlic cheese
1/8 tsp. Worcestershire sauce
chopped pecans

Soften cream cheese and blend in remaining ingredients except pecans. Shape into 1 or 2 balls and roll in chopped pecans. Refrigerate.

POOR MAN ALMOND BANKET

Set aside till room temperature, then mix:
1/2 lb. almond paste
2 eggs
2 stick margarine

Combine:
2 c. sugar
2 c. flour

Gradually add small amount of dry ingredients to almond mixture. Continue until all dry ingredients are mixed. Place in 9 x 13 pan and bake at 325 degrees for 45 minutes.

"TRIPLE BOGIE" TURKEY STUFFING

1 loaf bread broken into crumbs
2 tsp. salt
1/2 c. melted margarine
1/2 tsp. pepper
1 tsp. poultry seasoning
1 small onion – shopped
1 lb. pork sausage
1 c. hot milk
1 egg

Mix all ingredients together and stuff turkey.

- Trouble Shots: Learning to accept bad shots and the results are half the battle.
- Even though your ball may be buried in what you think is a substance that should have remained at the beach, or a 25-mile an hour headwind is blowing you off balance, always remember to go through your "Pre-swing Routine" before executing the shot.
- Learning to execute different shots is part of the game of golf, and taking a lesson may be the first step.

"MOM'S STICKS"
(BREAD AND BUTTER PICKLES)

Cover with brine of 1 c. salt to 9 c. water and let stand for 3 hours. Drain.

6 qt. (24 cups) cucumbers, washed and sliced
4 c. onions, sliced & cut in small pieces

In large pan, heat almost to boiling.

6 c. vinegar
6 c. sugar
1 tbsp. turmeric
1 tsp. mustard seed
1 tsp. celery seed
pickles and onion

Fill jars with pickles then fill with juice and seal. To seal: warm "Ball" lids in heated water to soften rubber around edges. Place lids on jars, then screw down tops. Let stand overnight. Lids should pop when they seal.

- **Lie of the Ball:** This should be your first consideration. When walking up to the ball, observe the lie. Is the ball sitting up, in the rough, in a sand trap, or under a tree? Each of these situations and others call for some thinking on your part regarding club selection.

Breads, Rolls, & Muffins

"ACE" BANANA BREAD

3 very ripe bananas
1/2 c. white sugar
1/2 c. brown sugar
1/2 c. melted margarine
1 egg
3 tbsp. cold water
2 1/2 c. flour
1 tsp. baking powder
1 tsp. baking soda dissolved in 1 tbsp. hot water
dash of salt

Mash bananas and let stand for 20 minutes. Mix remaining ingredients together in order. Blend in bananas and place in greased loaf pans. Bake at 375 degrees for 45 - 60 minutes. Cool before removing.

"STARTING-TIME" POPPY SEED BREAD

1 pkg. yellow cake mix
1 pkg. instant toasted coconut pudding mix
1/4 c. poppy seed
4 eggs
1/2 c. oil
1 c. hot water

Mix all ingredients together and pour into 2 greased loaf pans. Bake at 350 degrees for 40-45 minutes. Cool and remove from pans.

"EAGLE" CINNAMON BREAD

Bread Mix:
1 egg
1 c. sugar
1/4 c. oil
1/2 tsp. salt
1 tsp. baking soda
1 c. buttermilk
2 c. flour

Layer Mix:
1 tbsp. cinnamon
1/2 c. sugar

Mix all "bread mix" ingredients together with mixer until smooth. Pour a layer of batter into greased pan, sprinkle with cinnamon sugar, alternating until all is used up. Bake at 350 degrees for 1 hour.

WHOLE-WHEAT NUT SPICE BREAD

1 c. all-purpose flour
2 tsp. baking powder
1/4 tsp. salt
1/4 tsp. cinnamon
1/4 tsp. nutmeg
1/4 tsp. all-spice
1/2 c. whole-wheat flour
1/4 c. margarine
3/4 c. sugar
2 eggs
2/3 c. milk
1/2 tsp. vanilla
1/2 c. nuts – chopped

Sift together first 6 ingredients. Stir in whole-wheat flour.
Cream together margarine and sugar. Add eggs one
at a time, beating well after each addition.
Add dry ingredients alternately with milk and vanilla to
creamed mixture; beat smooth after each addition.
Stir in nuts. Turn into greased loaf pan and bake at 350
degrees for 55 minutes or until done. Cool 10 minutes;
remove from pan.

DATE BREAD

1 c. cut-up dates
1/2 tsp. baking soda
1/2 c. margarine
1 c. sugar
1 3/4 c. flour
1 tsp. baking powder
1 egg
dash of salt

Mix dates with 1 c. boiling water and baking soda. Cool. Add remaining ingredients and mix. Pour into greased bread pan and bake at 375 degrees for 45 - 60 minutes.

BREAD PUDDING – CUSTARD STYLE

3 slices bread
2 c. milk
3 eggs
1 c. sugar
1/2 tsp. salt
1 tsp. vanilla

Break bread into small pieces and soak in milk. In separate bowl, beat eggs with sugar. Blend in salt and vanilla and stir into bread mix. Bake in 2-quart casserole at 375 degrees for 45 - 60 minutes until brown and set like custard.

REFRIGERATOR ROLLS

1 pkg. dry active yeast
2 eggs
1/2 c. sugar
1 tsp. salt
5 tbsp. margarine
5 c. sifted flour

Dissolve yeast in 1/2 c. warm water and set aside. Then beat eggs and add sugar, salt, margarine and 1 c. warm water. Add yeast to this and beat 3 minutes. Stir in flour. Cover and set in refrigerator for 2 - 3 hours or over-night. Form into balls* and place on greased cookie sheet. Cover with towels in warm area until doubled in size. Bake at 350 degrees for 20 minutes.

Practicing the Sand Shot at Home:
- You can practice the most feared shot in golf at home with no one watching you.
- Using a plastic ball, practice hitting out of a sandbox, or build yourself a little area and put some sand in it.
- Remember: Use a full swing and **follow-through**, don't stop your swing when hitting out of the sand. Tip: It's like taking a slice of bread from under your ball.

CHERRY BREAD

3/4 c. oil
3/4 c. applesauce - natural
2 c. sugar
3 c. flour
1 tsp. almond extract
1 tsp. salt
1 tsp. baking soda
3 eggs
1 can cherry pie filling**

Mix together pour into 2 nonstick loaf pans. Bake at 350 degrees for 60 – 70 minutes.

** May substitute any flavor pie filling.

"OUT-OF-BOUNDS" ZUCCHINI BREAD

1 1/2 c. flour
1 1/2 c. whole-wheat flour
1 1/2 c. sugar
1 c. walnuts – chopped
4 1/2 tsp. baking powder
1 tsp. salt
4 eggs
2/3 c. oil
2 c. zucchini – grated
2 tsp. grated lemon peel
2 tsp. cinnamon
2 tsp. vanilla extract

In large bowl, with fork, mix first 6 ingredients. In medium bowl, beat eggs slightly and stir in the next 5 ingredients. Stir egg mixture into flour mixture just until flour is moistened. Spread evenly into 2 greased loaf pans. Bake at 350 degrees for 1 hour. Cool and remove from pans.

- **Hitting Out of the Rough:** Thick grass has a tendency to grab and open the clubface as you swing. To compensate for this, close your clubface at address.
- Also, do not ground your club; it might get caught in the grass, and throw your timing and swing off.

"BUNKER" BUNS

4 cans biscuits
Biscuit mix:
3/4 c. sugar
1 Tbsp. Cinnamon
1/2 c. chopped nuts

Topping:
1-1/2 sticks margarine
1 c. sugar

Cut biscuits in quarters and roll in biscuit mix. Place in
bundt pan. Melt margarine and add l c. sugar. Pour
over biscuits. Bake 40 min. at 350 degrees. Turn upside
down onto serving dish.

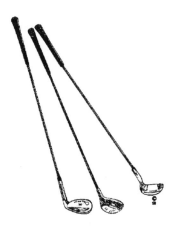

FOOD PROCESSOR BANANA BREAD

In food processor add:
2 bananas cut into 1 inch pieces
1/2 c. butter (chilled) cut into 6 pieces

Cover, process and chop for 20 seconds

Add:
1 1/2 c. flour
3/4 c. sugar
2 eggs
1/4 c. milk
2 tsp. lemon juice
1 tsp. baking soda
1/2 tsp. salt

Process for 10 seconds and pour into bread pan. Bake 1 hour at 350 degrees. Do not double.

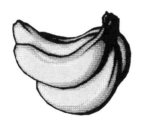

MOM'S ZUCCHINI BREAD

3 eggs - beaten until foamy
2 c. sugar
1 c. oil
2 c. grated zucchini
3 c. flour
1 tsp. salt
1/4 tsp. baking powder
1 tsp. baking soda
2-3 tsp. cinnamon
2-3 tsp. vanilla

Mix eggs, sugar, oil, and zucchini and set aside. Mix together remaining ingredients and add to zucchini mixture. Pour into 2 greased bread pans. Bake at 350 degrees for 1 hour.

**Optional Topping:
2 c. powdered sugar
3 oz. cream cheese
1 tbsp. milk
1 tsp. vanilla

Combine and spread on cooled bread.

CHOCOLATE ZUCCHINI BREAD

3 eggs
1 c. oil
2 c. sugar
1 tsp. vanilla
2 c. zucchini – peeled & shredded
2 1/2 c. flour
1/2 c. baking cocoa
1 tsp. salt
1 tsp. baking soda
1 tsp. cinnamon
1/4 tsp. baking powder

In bowl beat eggs, oil, sugar and vanilla. Stir in zucchini. In separate bowl combine dry ingredients and add to zucchini mixture and mix well. Pour and divide into 2 nonstick loaf pans. Bake at 350 degrees for 1 hour or until done.

- **Chipping Downhill:**
- Play the ball almost off your back foot.
- Use a lofted club
- If the pin is close to the edge of the green, chip the ball short of the green and use the grass or the fringe as a backstop, slowing the momentum of the ball so it will not roll over the green.

CINNAMON BREAD

1 egg
1 c. sugar
1/4 c. oil
1/2 tsp. salt
1 tsp. baking soda
1 c. buttermilk
2 c. flour

Mix all ingredients together and set aside.

Mix:
1 tbsp. cinnamon
1/2 c. sugar

Pour layer of dough into loaf pan, sprinkle with sugar and cinnamon mix. Alternate layers until all is used. Bake at 350 degrees for 1 hour. Makes one loaf.

- **Club Selection for Head Wind:**
  10 mph - 1 to 2 clubs more
  20 mph - 2 to 3 clubs more
  30 mph - 3 to 5 clubs more

"FIRST PLACE" RAISIN BRAN MUFFINS

In large bowl mix:
5 c. flour
2 tsp. salt
3 c. sugar
5 tsp. baking soda

In another bowl mix:
4 eggs – slightly beaten with fork
1/2 c. oil
1/2 c. applesauce - natural
1 qt. buttermilk (shake well)

15 oz. box "Post" Raisin Bran (Post brand works the best)

Add wet mixture to the flour mixture and stir well. Then add box of raisin bran. Mix well and refrigerate overnight. Will keep several weeks. Make muffins when you want them!

To bake: fill paper-lined or greased muffin cups to the top. Bake at 400 degrees for 20 – 25 minutes.
Optional: for a crunchy top, sprinkle with raw sugar just before baking – YUM !

Cakes,
Cookies
&
Desserts

"DIVOT" PIE (VARIATION OF MUD PIE)

1/2 pkg. chocolate wafers
1/2 stick margarine, melted
1/2 gal. chocolate ice cream
1/2 gal. coffee ice cream
1 1/2 c. fudge sauce
whipped cream
slivered almonds or chopped pecans

Crush wafers and add butter. Mix well and press into 9-inch pie plate. Soften ice cream and mix together, then cover pie crust and freeze until firm. Top with fudge sauce and place in freezer for 8 - 10 hours or until hard. Serve with whip cream and nuts.

- **Hitting Out of a Divot:** Do not change anything in your stance or ball position.
- Hit down on the ball slightly more than normal. This can be achieved by a more upright backswing.
- Imagine hitting a divot out of a divot.

"RAINED-OUT" COFFEE CAKE

Topping:
1 c. brown sugar
4 tbsp. melted margarine
4 tsp. cinnamon
1 c. nuts – chopped
4 tbsp. flour

Mix and set aside.

Cake mix:
<u>**Sift together:**</u>
3 c. sifted flour
6 tsp. baking powder
1/2 tsp. salt
1 1/2 c. sugar

<u>**Cut in:**</u>
1/2 c. margarine - softened
2 eggs – beaten
1 1/2 c. milk

Layer half of batter in large cake pan (9x13x2) then half of topping, followed by remaining batter. Top with rest of topping mix and bake at 350 degrees for 25 - 30 minutes.

"SECOND-CUT" REFRIGERATOR COOKIES

2 eggs
1 c. sugar
1 c. brown sugar
1 1/2 c. margarine
1 c. chopped walnuts
2 tbsp. boiling water
1 tsp. baking soda
1/2 tsp. salt
4 c. flour

Mix all ingredients together and form into loaf approximately 3" wide and 2" high. Freeze* or refrigerate overnight. Slice to desired thickness and bake at 400 degrees for 8 - 10 minutes or until golden brown.

* Freezing makes the dough easier to slice and allows you to use only the amount you wish.

"FAST PLAY" FRESH PEACH PIE

5 c. peaches – peeled & sliced
3/4 c. sugar
2 - 3 tbsp. flour
1/4 tsp. cinnamon
2 tbsp. margarine

Combine all ingredients. Put in double crust (shell and top) and bake at 400 degrees for 45 - 50 minutes.

"CHAMPION" COOKIE SANDWICHES
(My all time favorite)

Cookie mix:
1 c. margarine
1/3 c. evaporated milk
2 c. flour
1/2 tsp. salt

Mix and refrigerate 1 hour or more. Roll out to 1/8" to 1/4" thick and cut into quarter-size circles. Place on baking sheet and sprinkle half with colored sugar sprinkles. Bake at 325 degrees for 10 minutes. Watch closely.

Filling:
1/4 c. margarine – room temperature
1 c. powdered sugar
1 egg yolk

Mix and spread filling on each plain cookie and top with sugar sprinkled cookie.

"ORANGE BALL" ORANGE CAKE

**May substitute lemon jello and juice instead of orange to make lemon cake.

1 pkg. white cake mix
1 pkg. orange jello
4 eggs
3/4 c. oil
3/4 c. water

Combine all ingredients and mix for 5 – 6 minutes. Pour into nonstick cake pan and bake at 350 degrees for 45 - 60 minutes or until done. While hot, pierce cake with a fork and pour on "Glaze".

Glaze mix:
Combine:
1/2 c. orange juice
2 c. powdered sugar

"SLICE & HOOK " FRUIT PIZZA

1 roll sugar cookie dough
8 oz. cream cheese
8 oz. cool whip
bananas
grapes
apples
strawberry's
any type fruit you like

Press cookie dough flat and spread with oil. Bake at
325 degrees for 10 minutes or until golden brown. Let
cool. Blend cream cheese and cool whip and spread
on top of cookie dough. Slice your favorite fruits and
decorate.

**Optional – Glaze for topping
1 c. orange juice
2 tbsp. corn starch
1 tsp. lemon juice
sweeten with sugar to desired taste

Boil till thick. Cool before pouring on fruit.

- **Slicing the Ball:**
- **Causes:** Feet in an open stance, clubface in an open
  position, or a weak grip.
- **Cures:** Square your stance, square the clubface, and
  move your grip to a slightly stronger position.

MIKE'S DELUXE CHOCOLATE MARSHMALLOW BARS

3/4 c. margarine
1 1/2 c. sugar
3 eggs
1 tsp. vanilla
1 1/3 c. flour
1/2 tsp. baking powder
1/2 tsp. salt
3 tbsp. cocoa
1/2 c. chopped nuts
4 c. marshmallows

Cream margarine and sugar. Add eggs and vanilla, beat until fluffy. Combine flour, baking powder, salt, and cocoa and add to cream mix. Stir in nuts. Bake at 350 degrees for 15 - 18 minutes. Put marshmallows on and bake an additional 2 - 3 minutes. Spread with knife dipped in water. Cool

Topping:
1 1/3 c. (8oz) chocolate chips
3 tbsp. margarine
1 c. peanut butter
2 c. rice crispy cereal

Combine chocolate chips, margarine and peanut butter in small pan. Cook stirring constantly until well blended. Remove and stir in cereal. Spread on baked bars. May freeze.

CHEESECAKE BROWNIES

1 pkg. fudge brownie mix
8 oz. cream cheese-softened
1/3 – 1/2 c. sugar
1 egg
1/2 tsp. vanilla

Combine and prepare brownie mix as directed and put in 9 X 13 pan.
Beat cream cheese with electric mixer till smooth. Add sugar, egg and vanilla and mix until blended. Pour over brownie mix and cut through batter with knife for marbled effect.
Bake at 350 degrees for 35 - 40 min.
Cool and cut into squares.

BLUEBERRY DELIGHT

1 c. graham cracker crumbs
1/4 stick margarine
1 pkg. (8 oz) cream cheese
2 eggs
1/2 c. sugar
1 can blueberry pie filling
whipped cream

Mix crumbs and margarine and line bottom of 9 x 9 pan. Beat cream cheese, eggs, and sugar and pour on top of crumbs. Bake for 15 min. at 350 degrees. Cool in refrigerator. Pour blueberry pie filling over crumbs, and top with cool whip or whipped cream.

DAD'S APPLE PIE

2 pie shells (unbaked)
6 apples (Macintosh preferred) peeled and sliced
1 c. sugar
1 1/2 tsp. cinnamon
1/2 tsp. nutmeg
1/8 tsp. salt
1/8 tsp. lemon juice
2 Tbsp. margarine

Fill pie shell with apples. Mix sugar, cinnamon, nutmeg, salt, and lemon juice together. Then sprinkle mixture on apples, dot with butter and cover with pie shell and bake at 425 degrees for 30 – 40 minutes.

- Getting More From a Golf Lesson:
- Arrive a few minutes early and warm-up.
- Have an open mind to changes and suggestions and let the instructor know what you are having problems with.
- And finally, not all professionals teach the same way, find one that is right for you.

DUTCH COOKIES

2 sticks margarine
2/3 c. brown sugar
2/3 c. sugar
1 egg
1 tsp. vanilla
1 tbsp. almond extract
2 c. flour

Combine in bowl and beat until smooth. Place in greased muffin pans (24) and bake at 350 degrees for 15 minutes – watch. Cool for 3 minutes and flip out.

"CHERRY HILLS" CHEESE PIE

1 1/2 c. graham cracker crumbs
2/3 c. melted margarine
2 eggs
8 oz. pkg. cream cheese
1/4 c. sugar
22 oz. can cherry pie filling
whipped cream

Combine cracker crumbs and margarine, and pat into pie pan. Beat eggs, cream cheese, and sugar. Pour over crust. Bake at 325 degrees for 20 min. Spoon pie filling over the top and chill.

*Serve with whipped cream or ice cream.

EASY CUP CAKES

3 1/3 c. flour
2 c. sugar
1/2 tsp. salt
5 tsp. baking powder
2/3 c. margarine – melted
1 1/3 c. milk
2 eggs
2 tsp. vanilla

Mix all ingredients together and pour into muffin tins with paper cupcake liners. Bake at 350 degrees for 20 – 30 minutes or until golden brown.

** This recipe is doubled. I use what I need and freeze the rest.

"WATER HAZARD" BLUEBERRY PIE

2 1/2 c. fresh blueberries
1 c. sugar
1/4 c. flour
1/8 tsp. salt
1 tbsp. lemon juice
3 tbsp. margarine
8" unbaked pie shell, plus top shell

Combine first 5 ingredients. Fill unbaked pie shell and cover with second pie shell. Cut 1" slits in top and dot with margarine. Sprinkle with sugar and bake at 450 degrees for 10 minutes, then at 375 degrees for 40 minutes.

- Hitting Out of a Water Hazard: Use a lofted club, preferably a pitching wedge but nothing less than a 9-iron. You need the cutting action that comes when you use a lofted club with an open clubface.
- And use the same swing as for the full sand shot.
- Expect to get wet.

SOUR CREAM POUND CAKE

2 sticks margarine
3 c. sugar
1 c. sour cream
6 eggs
3 c. flour – sifted with baking soda 3 times
1/4 tsp. baking soda
1 tsp. vanilla

Cream margarine and sugar well. Add eggs (one at a time) and alternate with sour cream and flour. In large tube pan, bake at 325 degrees for 55 - 65 minutes or until toothpick comes out clean.

STRAWBERRY CAKE

1 pkg. white cake mix
1 pkg. strawberry jello
1/2 pkg. frozen strawberries
1/2 c. water
2/3 c. oil
4 eggs

Mix all together and place in tube pan. Bake at 350 degrees for 50 minutes or until done. Frost with topping of choice.

BLUEBERRY CREAM CHEESE PIE

2 pie crusts
3 small bananas
8 oz. pkg. cream cheese
1 c. sugar
2 - 8 oz. cool whip
1 can blueberry pie filling
1/4 c. nuts-chopped fine
lemon juice

Press chopped nuts between unbaked pie crusts and pat crust together. Bake at 350 degrees for 8 – 10 minutes or until done. Slice bananas and sprinkle with lemon juice. Place on bottom of pie crusts. Mix cream cheese, sugar, and one - 8 oz. cool whip until stiff. Spread over bananas. Top with blueberry filling and cover with remaining cool whip.

** Can substitute any pie filling.

PUMPKIN DESSERT

Crust:
1 c. flour
1/2 c. margarine
1/4 c. sugar

Mix and pat in 9 x 9" pan. Bake at 425 degrees for 10 – 15 minutes and cool.

Filling:
1 pkg. instant vanilla pudding
2/3 c. milk
1 c. pumpkin
1/2 tsp. cinnamon
1/4 tsp. ginger
8 oz. non-dairy whipped topping

Beat first 5 ingredients at medium speed until well mixed. Stir in whipped topping. Pour over crust and refrigerate.

"SUDDEN DEATH"
NESTLE CRUNCH ICE CREAM DESSERT

1/2 gal. vanilla ice cream – softened
3 Nestle Crunch candy bars – crushed
2 tbsp. peanut butter
10 graham cracker squares – crushed

Options:

Option 1: Mix all together and refreeze.

Option 2: Mix candy bars, peanut butter, and crackers. Pat on bottom of dish and pour softened ice cream over the top and refreeze.

- Sudden Death: A type of play-off in which play continues until one of the players scores less than his or her opponent.

MICROWAVE CARROT SPICE CAKE

1 1/2 c. flour
2 tsp. cinnamon
1 tsp. baking soda
1/2 tsp. salt
1 1/2 c. sugar
1 c. cooking oil
3 eggs
2 tsp. vanilla
2 c. grated raw carrots
1/2 c. nuts – chopped (optional)

Mix together flour, cinnamon, baking soda and salt.
Combine sugar, oil, eggs and vanilla in large mixing
bowl. Blend at low mixing speed for 30 seconds. Add
dry ingredients. Mix at medium speed for 3 minutes.
Fold in carrots and nuts. Pour into 2-quart casserole
dish. Cover with paper towel and microwave on high
for 12 - 15 minutes. Turn halfway through cooking.
When toothpick comes out clean, cake is done.
Immediately remove paper towel. Let cool.

BECKY'S LEMON TEA CAKES

1 1/2 tsp. vinegar
1/2 c. milk
1/2 c. margarine
3/4 c. sugar
1 egg
1 tsp. shredded lemon peel
1 3/4 c. sifted flour
1 tsp. baking powder
1/4 tsp. baking soda
1/4 tsp. salt

Lemon Glaze:
3/4 c. sugar
1/4 c. lemon juice

Stir vinegar into milk. Cream margarine and sugar until fluffy. Beat in egg and lemon peel. Sift dry ingredients and add to creamed mixture alternately with milk, and beat after each addition.
Drop from a teaspoon 2 inches apart on ungreased cookie sheet. Bake at 350 degrees for 12 – 14 minutes. Remove at once and brush with lemon glaze. Makes about 4 dozen little cake-like cookies.

"MATCH-PLAY" CHERRY CRUNCH

1 c. quick-cooking oats
1 c. flour
3/4 c. brown sugar
1/2 tsp. cinnamon
1/2 c. margarine
1 (22 oz.) can cherry pie filling

Combine oats, flour, sugar, and cinnamon in bowl. Cut in margarine with fork until particles are fine. Spread half the mixture in 9" square baking pan. Cover with pie filling and sprinkle with remaining oat mixture. Bake at 375 degrees for 40 minutes.

- Flyers: The results and characteristics of a ball that is hit from a soft lie in the rough. Usually resulting in a longer than normal shot.

SELF-FILLED CHOCOLATE CUPCAKES
(Good luck eating just one!)

1 pkg. chocolate cake mix
8 oz. cream cheese
1/3 c. sugar
dash of salt
1 egg
6 oz. chocolate chips

Mix cake mix according to directions. In small bowl mix cream cheese, sugar, salt and egg. Line muffin tins with paper cupcake liners. Fill 2/3 full with cake mix. Drop 1 rounded tsp. cream cheese mix on top of each cup cake along with 4 - 6 chocolate chips. Bake at 350 degrees for 20 - 30 minutes.

MARY'S CHEESECAKE

Crust:
2 c. crushed graham crackers
1/4 lb. margarine, (1 stick) melted
3/4 c. sugar

Mix and pat into 9 x 13 pan.

Filling:
16 oz. cream cheese, room temperature
4 tbsp. margarine, room temperature
1 c. sugar
2 eggs
4 tbsp. flour
2 tbsp. lemon juice

Cream together cream cheese and margarine. Add
remaining ingredients. Mix well and pour over crust.
Bake at 350 degrees for 35 minutes. Cool and
refrigerate overnight.

Putting Tip:
- Putting is the area where the least amount of time is
  spent practicing but where the most strokes are
  accumulated.
- Before you putt, set a goal for each putt and stick to
  it.

FRESH PEACH DESSERT

2 1/2 c. fresh peaches - sliced
3/4 c. sugar
4 tbsp. margarine
1/2 tsp. salt
1 tsp. baking powder
1 c. flour
1/2 c. milk

1 c. sugar
1 tbsp. cornstarch
1/8 tsp. salt
1/2 tsp. cinnamon

Butter an 8 x 8 pan and cover bottom with sliced peaches. Cream 3/4 c. sugar and margarine; set aside. Sift 1/2 tsp. salt, baking powder and flour together. Add to cream mixture with the milk and spread over peaches. In a small bowl, mix 1 c. sugar, cornstarch, 1/8 tsp. salt and cinnamon. Sprinkle over batter. Pour 1 c. boiling water over everything. Bake at 350 degrees for 1 hour.

PEACH BUTTERSCOTCH PIE
(First pie I ever made!)

6 small fresh or canned peach halves
3/4 c. brown sugar
1/2 tsp. salt
3 tbsp. flour
1/3 c. light corn syrup
1 tbsp. lemon juice
1/3 c. margarine
1/8 tsp. almond extract
2 unbaked pie shells

Place peaches cut side-up on bottom of unbaked pie shell. In medium pan, mix and heat next 6 ingredients 1 - 2 minutes; add extract. Cool slightly and pour over peaches. Top with pie shell and bake at 450 degrees for 15 minutes, then reduce heat and bake at 375 degrees for 30 minutes.

CINNAMON SUGAR COOKIES

1 c. soft margarine
1 1/2 c. sugar
2 eggs
2 3/4 c. sifted flour
2 tsp. cream of tartar
1 tsp. baking soda
1/4 tsp. salt

Mix together margarine, sugar, and eggs. Sift together flour, cream of tartar, baking soda and salt. Stir into margarine mix. Shape into walnut-size balls. Roll in mix of: !/4 c. sugar and 2 tsp. cinnamon. Place on ungreased cookie sheet and bake at 400 degrees for 8 – 10 minutes.

"GROUND-UNDER REPAIR" PEANUT BUTTER COOKIES

1 c. brown sugar
1/2 c. margarine
2 c. flour
1/2 tsp. salt
1 c. sugar
1 c. peanut butter
2 eggs
2 tsp. baking soda

Mix in order. Roll in balls and press flat with floured fork on greased cookie sheet. Bake at 375 degrees for 8 – 10 minutes.

FLORIDA OATMEAL COOKIES

1 egg white
1 c. sugar
1 c. soft margarine
1 c. plus 3 tbsp. flour
1 tsp. baking soda
1 tsp. vanilla
2 c. uncooked oatmeal
1/2 c. nuts - chopped

Mix all ingredients together. Form into walnut-sized balls and place on lightly greased cookie sheet. Bake at 350 degrees for 10 – 12 minutes.

"CLASSIC SWING" SUGAR COOKIES
**This is a double batch.

Cream together:
2 c. margarine
3 c. sugar
3 eggs
2 tsp. vanilla
1 c. sour cream
1 c sweet cream

Beat well and set aside.

Sift together:
1 tsp. baking soda
4 tsp. baking powder
10 c. flour

Add to cream mixture and form into cookie balls. Place on greased cookie sheet and bake at 350 degrees until golden brown.

"WARM-UP" HONEY BUN CAKE

1 box yellow cake mix
3/4 c. oil
4 eggs
1 tsp. vanilla
8 oz. sour cream

Mix and pour in 11 x 13 pan.

In separate bowl, mix:
1 c. brown sugar
3 tsp. cinnamon

Sprinkle over cake and swirl with a fork. Bake at 325 degrees for 40 – 45 minutes.

Icing:
2 c. confectioners sugar
1 tsp. vanilla
4 tsp. milk

Mix together and pour over baked, hot cake.

- **Warming-Up Before you Play:** Arrive at the course early, and take your time.
- Hit a bucket of balls starting with short chip shots and ending by practicing some putts.
- DO NOT work on your swing.

"SOUTHERN PLANTATION" PEACH COBBLER

4 c. peaches – peeled and sliced
1/2 c. butter
1 c. flour
1 c. sugar
1/2 tsp. cinnamon
3/4 c. milk
2 tsp. baking powder
1/2 tsp. salt

Cook peaches in sugar water (2-tbsp. sugar) over medium heat until tender. In 9 x 13 pan, melt margarine. Drain peaches and place in buttered pan. In large bowl combine remaining ingredients and mix well. Pour batter over peaches and bake at 350 degrees for 55 - 65 minutes or until lightly browned.

- Practice Putting Tip: One of the best tips I got from a fellow golf instructor was to practice putting with my eyes on the target and not on the ball.
- This forces you to follow-through to your target and gets the putter head moving in the direction of the hole.
- This will help with your sense of direction.

Main Dishes

"CADDYSHACK" CHILI

Makes 6 qts. Freezes well.

3 lbs. ground chuck
2 large onions – chopped
2 large stalks celery – chopped
3 cans chili hot beans
3 pkgs. Chili-O chili seasoning
        (2 regular, 1 "hot" style)
1 – 2 tsp. chili powder (optional)
1 tsp. red pepper (optional)
3 large cans tomato sauce
2 cans kidney beans

Sauté ground chuck, onions and celery. Drain grease. Add rest of ingredients. Simmer until flavors are well blended.

To serve: Sprinkle with **shredded cheese** and onions.

"HAZARD" HAMBURGER STEW

1 1/2 lbs. lean ground beef
4 large potatoes – diced
1 medium onion – diced
4 carrots – sliced
1/4 c. flour
salt and pepper

Brown ground beef in large skillet or Dutch oven. Drain excess fat. Add vegetables and sprinkle flour on top. Add water just to cover and stir. Let simmer about 1 hour till vegetables are tender and stew has thickened. Season to taste. Serves 4 – 6.

**May add "Kitchen Bouquet" to brown.

- **Course Management:** The strategic placement of shots in order to take advantage of the layout of the hole and golf course.
- **One suggestion:** It is not necessary to aim for the flagstick on every hole!

"DIMPLE" CHILI-CON-CARNE

1 lb. lean ground beef
1 medium onion – chopped
1 green pepper – chopped
1 lb. can tomatoes – broken up
8 oz. can tomato sauce
1 lb. can chili beans, drained
1 tsp. salt
2 tsp. chili powder (to taste)
1 bay leaf

In heavy skillet or Dutch oven, cook ground beef until lightly browned, drain off grease. Add onion, and green pepper, cook until tender. Stir in remaining ingredients. Cover and simmer for 1 hour. Remove bay leave. Serves 4 – 6.

"HOLE-IN-ONE" MACARONI AND CHEESE

6 tbsp. margarine
1/4 c. flour
1 tsp. salt
1/2 tsp. dry mustard
1/4 tsp. pepper
3/4 tsp. Worcestershire sauce
3 c. milk
1 tsp. instant minced onion
3/4 lb. sharp cheddar cheese, shredded
2 c. elbow macaroni, cooked and drained
3/4 c. soft bread crumbs

In saucepan melt 4-tbsp. margarine; blend in flour and
seasonings. Gradually stir in milk; cook and stir until
thick and smooth. Stir in onions and cheese. Pour over
cooked macaroni in greased 2-quart casserole dish
and mix lightly. Melt remaining margarine and mix with
bread crumbs. Sprinkle over macaroni. Bake at 375
degrees for 30 - 35 minutes or until golden brown.

- The Backswing: When taking a backswing remember
  to keep it low and slow.
- The first movement in your swing is with your hands,
  arms, and shoulders working as one unit.

QUICK AND EASY CURRIED CHICKEN

1 lb. chicken filets cut into 1" cubes
1/2 c. celery, chopped
1/2 c. apples, chopped and peeled
2 tbsp. raisins
1 can cream of potato soup
1 c. milk
1-2 tbsp. curry powder, to taste
cooked rice

Quick-fry chicken cubes and set aside. In small bowl, mix soup, curry and milk; add to chicken and stir. Add remaining ingredients except rice and simmer about 20 - 30 minutes.
Serve over rice.

"PLAY-THROUGH" CHICKEN WITH RICE

In a large roaster, put **2 c. rice** (not instant) and 1 c. water.

Mix together and pour over rice:
3 tbsp. soy sauce
2 cans cream of celery soup
2 cans cream of mushroom soup

Place 2 cut-up chickens on top of soup mixture. **NO SALT.** Sprinkle **1 pkg. dry onion soup mix** over all. Cover **TIGHTLY** with **2 layers** of aluminum foil. DO NOT PEAK!!
Bake at 325 degrees for 3 hours. Serves 4-6

EASY STIR-FRY HOT DOGS

1 tsp. vegetable oil
1/4 c. onion – chopped
6 oz. hot dogs cut into 1" pieces
1/2 c. snow peas – blanched
1/2 c. carrots – blanched
1/3 c. sliced celery – blanched
3/4 c. canned pineapple chunks
1 tsp. soy sauce
1 tsp. cornstarch dissolved in 3 tbsp. warm water

In frying pan heat oil; add onion and sauté until tender. Add hot dogs and vegetables and cook 5 minutes, stirring constantly. Add pineapple and soy sauce; cook another 2 minutes. Add dissolved cornstarch, stir and cook until sauce thickens.

TACO SALAD MAIN DISH

1 1/2 lb. ground beef – cooked and drained
2 pkgs. taco mix
1 onion – chopped
6 oz. tortilla chips – crushed
2 tomatoes – diced
1 medium lettuce – shredded
8 oz. cheddar cheese – grated
1 small bottle 1000 island dressing.

Cook ground beef and add taco mix. Cool. Add remaining ingredients and toss. Refrigerate.

CREAMED CABBAGE AND HAM

1 tbsp. margarine
1/4 c. onions – chopped
1 garlic clove – minced
1 c. carrots – sliced thin
3 c. cabbage - thinly sliced and cut
6 oz. ham, cooked and cut into thin stripes
3 tbsp. flour
3/4 c. chicken broth
1/2 c. milk
1/4 tsp. nutmeg
dash of pepper

Melt margarine in skillet. Add onions and garlic and cook until translucent. Add carrots and stir-fry 3 minutes. Add cabbage and cook 10 minutes; stir in ham. Place flour in small bowl and gradually add broth; stir until smooth and add to ham mixture. Add milk, nutmeg, and pepper. Stir constantly for 3 minutes, until thick. Serve as desired.

"ON-THE-FAIRWAY" CHEESE STUFFED ZUCCHINI

2 zucchini, about 5 oz. each
2 tsp. oil
1 c. mushrooms – sliced
1 tsp. garlic – minced
4 oz. mozzarella cheese – shredded
1 tsp. dried basil
1 tbsp. fresh parsley – chopped
dash of salt, pepper, and nutmeg
4 tsp. grated Parmesan cheese

Cut ends off zucchini; slice each in half lengthwise and scoop out pulp, reserve shells and pulp. Heat oil in small saucepan; add pulp, mushrooms, and garlic. Sauté until all ingredients are soft. Transfer mix to a bowl and add cheese, basil, parsley, and seasonings; toss well. Spoon 1/4 of mix into each zucchini shell and arrange shells in baking dish. Top with Parmesan cheese. Cover and bake at 350 degrees for 30 minutes; remove cover and bake an additional 15 minutes.

CHILLED SUMMER SPAGHETTI WITH VEGETABLES AND CHICKEN

7 oz. thin spaghetti – cooked and cooled
1/2 c. mayonnaise
1/2 pkg. (8oz) frozen mixed vegetables - steamed and cooled
1/2 lb. chicken filets, cooked and cut into 1" cubes

Rinse cooked spaghetti thoroughly with cold water and drain. Place in 2-quart bowl. Add mayonnaise and mix. Fold in vegetables and chicken. Cool in refrigerator for 30 - 45 minutes. Serves 4

TEXAS HASH

2 large onions – diced
2 bell peppers – diced
1 lb. lean ground beef
2 c. tomatoes - chopped
1/2 c. uncooked rice
2 tsp. salt
1/2 tsp. pepper
1 tsp. chili powder

Brown hamburger and add onions and peppers. Cook until onions are clear. Add tomatoes, rice and seasoning. Mix and bake at 350 degrees for 45 minutes. Freezes well.

CARROT-POTATO "GOLF BAGS"
(Baked-stuffed potatoes)

4 small-medium baking potatoes
4-6 oz Neufchatel cheese, cut into chunks and
softened
4 tbsp. milk
1/3 tsp. salt
dash of pepper
1 c. carrots - cooked, chopped & pureed
3 tbsp. green onion - chopped
1/2 garlic glove - chopped very fine

Bake potatoes in 375-degree oven for 45 minutes. Cool slightly and cut in half lengthwise. Scoop out potatoes and place in small bowl. Reserve shells. Add cheese, milk, salt, pepper and beat until fluffy, adding milk as needed. Fold in carrot, garlic and green onion. Spoon mixture into potato shells and bake at 375-degrees for 12-15 minutes. Sprinkle with chives.

POTATO - CHEESE CASSEROLE

4 c. potatoes - peeled, cubed, and cooked
1 c. cream style cottage cheese
1 c. sour cream
1/3 c. green onions – chopped
1 tbsp. fresh parsley
1 garlic clove – minced
1/2 tsp. salt
1/3 - 1/2 c. shredded cheddar cheese
paprika

Set cooked and cubed potatoes aside. In large bowl combine next 6 ingredients and mix well. Stir in potatoes and place in lightly greased casserole. Bake at 350 degrees for 25 minutes. Top with cheese and sprinkle with paprika. Bake an additional 5 minutes or until cheese melts. Serves 6.

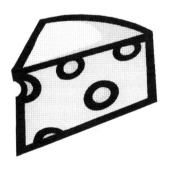

"HILLY LIE" CRESCENT BEEF POT PIE

1 boneless beef top sirloin, 3/4" thick
1/3 tsp. pepper
garlic salt
1 pkg. (16 oz) frozen potato, onion, red pepper mixture
3 tbsp. water
1/2 tsp. dried thyme leaves
1 jar (12 oz) mushroom gravy
1 can refrigerated crescent rolls

Cut steak into 2 or 3 strips then crosswise into 1/2" thick slices. Spray 10" <u>ovenproof</u> skillet with cooking spray. Heat until hot. Add beef and stir fry 1 minute. Remove from skillet and season with pepper and garlic salt.

In same skillet, combine frozen potato mixture, water and thyme. Cook and stir 3 minutes or until defrosted. Stir in gravy and bring to a boil. Remove from heat. Add beef to skillet and mix.

Separate crescent rolls into 8 triangles and roll up halfway. Arrange over beef mixture so pointed ends are directed toward center. Bake at 375 degrees for 17 – 20 minutes. Serves 4.

- Uphill Lie: Don't try to compensate for the hill by putting to much weight on your target side; go with the contour of the slope. Play the ball forward in your stance, and use one more club than normal.

"ORANGE BALL" CHICKEN

6 boneless chicken breasts, skinned
3 tbsp. margarine
1 tsp. paprika
1/4 tsp. pepper
1 (6oz) can frozen orange juice, thawed and undiluted
1 tsp. dried rosemary
1/2 tsp. dried thyme

Dot chicken with margarine and place on broiler rack.
Broil 3 - 5 minutes on each side or until golden brown.
Remove from oven and put into 9 x 13 pan. Sprinkle
with paprika and pepper. Pour juice over chicken and
sprinkle with remaining seasonings. Bake at 350
degrees for 30 minutes.

- **The Lag Putt:** A putt where a golfer attempts to get the ball close to the hole, not necessarily make the putt. Highly recommended on very long putts.
- Imagine a 3-foot circle around the hole. Try to "lag" the putt within this circle.

"SHOTGUN START" EGG-CHEESE CASSEROLE

Mix:
6 eggs
1/2 c. flour
2 tsp. sugar
1 c. milk
1/2 tsp. salt
1 tsp. baking powder

Mix and add to egg mixture:
1 lb. Monterey Jack cheese – cubed
1 (3 oz) pkg. cream cheese – cubed
12 oz. cottage cheese
3/4 stick oleo – cubed

Bake at 350 degrees in greased 2-quart casserole for 35 - 45 minutes.

- Shotgun Start: A means of starting a tournament in which there is a group of golfers starting on each hole at the same time. Play begins when you hear a shotgun fire, or a siren sound.

APPLE – CARROT DELIGHT

7 - 8 carrots scraped and diced
1/2 tsp. salt
1 can apple pie filling
1/2 c. sugar
margarine
paprika

Boil carrots in salt water until tender, then drain.
Combine apple pie filling and sugar. Mix in carrots and
place in casserole dish. Dot with margarine and
sprinkle with paprika. Bake at 375 degrees for 1 hour.

"SUNDAY BRUNCH" AT THE COURSE

3-6 crescent rolls
1 c. shredded cheddar cheese
1 lb. sausage - browned and drained

Mix together:
6 eggs
2 c. milk
1 tsp. dry mustard
1 tsp. salt

Line bottom of casserole pan with rolls, sausage, and
cheese. Pour mixture over above ingredients. Cover
and refrigerate overnight. Bake at 350 degrees for 45
minutes.

CHICKEN A-LA-SAM & BECKY

1 tbsp. margarine
1 tbsp. flour
1 cup milk
1/3 c. half and half
1 c. cooked chicken – chopped
1 tbsp. pimiento – chopped
1 /4 c. celery – diced
1 /4 c. carrots – diced
1/2 tsp. paprika
1/4 tsp. salt
1/8 tsp. pepper
toast, rice or noodles

Melt margarine in saucepan over low heat; add flour.
Cook 1 minute stirring constantly until smooth.
Gradually add milk and half-and-half and cook over
medium heat, stirring constantly until thickened. Stir
next 7 ingredients into the sauce. Cook until heated.
Serve over rice, rolls, or noodles. Serves 2 - 3.

"MOVEABLE OBSTRUCTION" LEMON CHICKEN FINGERS

1 lb. chicken tenderloins
1 tbsp. margarine
1/2 c. water
1/2 c. bottled Italian dressing

Sauce:
1 1/2 c. mayonnaise
1/4 c. lemon juice

In skillet, melt margarine. Add tenderloins and sauté until browned. Add water and cook to reduce to about 1/3 cup. Place chicken into ovenproof dish and cover with Italian dressing. Cover and bake at 350 degrees for 30 - 40 minutes. Cool slightly. Remove chicken and refrigerate until chilled or overnight. Before serving, mix sauce ingredients and spoon over chicken.

"FAST PLAY" GREEN BEAN DISH

2 cans french-style beans, drained
1 can cream of mushroom soup
1 can (small) french-fried onion rings
1/4 c. slivered almonds - optional
1/8 c. real bacon bits - optional

Mix beans, soup, almonds and bacon in a sauce pan.
Heat thoroughly. Stir in 1/2 can french-fried onions.
Heat for an additional 1 - 2 minutes. Serve and sprinkle
remaining french-fried onions on top.

- **To Speed Up Play:**
- **Place your bag or cart on the side of the green near the next hole, and not in front of the green.**
- **Be ready to hit your ball at all times.**
- **Finally, mark your score on the next tee box and not on the green.**

SNOW ON THE MOUNTAIN

Serve buffet style in containers or serving dishes that would best suit each ingredient. This unique recipe is very filling and fun to serve. Vary your amounts based on the number of persons in your party. Each ingredient is placed on top of the previous one, <u>in the following order,</u> to form a mountain with the coconut being the snow.

1. **cooked rice**
2. **chow mein noodles**
3. **cream chicken (2 chickens cooked and deboned. Mix 1 can cream of chicken soup, 1 can peas, dash of poultry seasoning, dash of pepper, and 1/4 c. milk. Heat and add chicken to mixture.)**
4. **tomatoes - chopped**
5. **celery – chopped**
6. **onions - chopped**
7. **sharp cheddar cheese – shredded**
8. **slivered almonds**
9. **crushed pineapple**
10. **coconut – "Snow on the Mountain"**

Have fun and be creative.

"SHORT BACKSWING" PIZZA CASSEROLE

2 lb. lean ground beef
1/4 c. green pepper – diced
2 cans cream of mushroom soup
2 cans tomato soup with 1/2 c. water
4 oz. can mushrooms
1/2 tsp. garlic powder
1/2 tsp. oregano
5 oz. pepperoni, sliced and quartered
dash of basil leaves
dash of salt
2 c. noodles
12 oz. shredded mozzarella cheese

Cook noodles in salted water, and drain. Brown ground beef and green peppers together. Combine next 8 ingredients and mix in beef and green peppers. Layer noodles, meat mixture, and cheese in greased casserole, ending with cheese. Bake at 325 degrees for 30 – 40 minutes.
Serves 8 – 10.

" LEFTHANDED" TURKEY OR CHICKEN HOT DISH

1st layer
3 c. cooked turkey or chicken
2 c. soft bread – cubed
1 c. celery – diced
1 small onion – diced
1/2 tsp. salt
1/4 tsp. paprika

Mix and spread on bottom of 9 x 13 pan.

2nd layer
4 eggs, beaten
1 c. milk
1 c. chicken broth
1 can cream of mushroom soup
2 tbsp. margarine

Mix and pour over 1st layer. Bake at 350 degrees for 1 hour.

"LADIES CLUB" SCALLOPED POTATOES

1 can cream of celery soup
3/4 c. milk
dash pepper
4 c. sliced potatoes
1 small onion – diced
1 c. shredded sharp cheddar cheese
1 tbsp. margarine
dash paprika

Combine soup, milk, and pepper in bowl. In buttered 2-quart casserole, arrange <u>layers</u> of potatoes, onion, soup sauce and cheese. Dot top with margarine and sprinkle with paprika. Cover and bake at 375 degrees for 1 hour. Serves 6

POTATO PANCAKES

4-6 potatoes – peeled and grated
2 eggs beaten
1 tbsp. sweet onion – chopped
1 tsp. salt
1 1/2 c. heavy cream**
1/4 c. flour – as needed

Combine all ingredients in large bowl and mix together well. Cook as desired on baking skillet. Brown on both sides.

** For fun: use 1 c. heavy cream and 1/2 c. chocolate milk. Kids will love it.

"GREAT SHOT" HOT DISH

2-3 c. cooked chicken or turkey cubed
2 cans cream of chicken soup
3 hard-boiled eggs - chopped
1 c. celery - chopped
2 tsp. onion or 1/2 small - chopped
1 can carrots – drain
1 can french style green beans – drained
1/2 c. mayonnaise

Mix all ingredients together and place in casserole dish. Top with crushed **potato chips**. Bake at 350 degrees for 45 minutes.

CHICKEN CASSSEROLE

2 cans cream of mushroom soup
2 1/2 c. milk
1/2 lb. processed American cheese - cubed
4 c. cooked chicken or turkey
7 oz. cooked macaroni
3 hard boiled eggs – chopped
1/2 c. margarine
1 1/2 c. soft bread crumbs

In large bowl combine soup, milk, and cheese. Add chicken, macaroni and eggs. Stir in 1/4 c. melted margarine. Put in 9 x 13 dish, cover and refrigerate 8 hours or overnight. Toss bread crumbs with remaining margarine and sprinkle on top of casserole. Bake at 350 degrees for 60 - 65 minutes. Yields 10 - 12 servings

"SLOW PLAY" PORK CHOPS

4-6 pork chops or cutlets
1/4 c. brown sugar
1/2 tsp. cinnamon
1/4 tsp. ground cloves
2 cup spaghetti sauce
1/4 cup vinegar

Brown pork shops in skillet and pour off excess fat.
Mix: brown sugar, cinnamon, cloves, spaghetti sauce,
and vinegar.
Pour 1/3 of mixture on bottom of slow cooker, then
arrange pork shops on top. Pour remaining mixture
over pork chops. Cover and cook on low for 4 - 6 hours.

* I serve this with rice.

"GREEN SIDE" CREAMY CHICKEN DEVILED EGG CASSEROLE

8 eggs deviled with:
1/3 c. mayonnaise
1/2 tsp. salt
1/2 tsp. curry powder
1/2 tsp. paprika
1 tsp. mustard

Mix together:
1 small can chicken (drained)
1 can cream of chicken soup
8 oz. sour cream
milk may be added to dilute mixture

Pour mixture over deviled eggs in casserole dish. Sprinkle with bread crumbs or potato chips. Bake at 350 degrees for 20 min.

- **Putting From Off the Green:** If the grass is not too long, I would putt anytime instead of chipping. If you don't have to hit a ball in the air, don't.
- Remember that a bad putt is still better than a bad chip.

"CHEESEBURGER-IN-PARADISE" CASSEROLE

1 lb. ground beef
1 small onion and bell pepper - chopped
1 tsp. salt
1/2 tsp. black pepper
1/2 c. water
8 oz. tomato paste
8 slices of cheese
1 can biscuits

Brown ground beef, onions and peppers. Drain. Add
tomato paste and water, simmer. Spoon into casserole
dish and place biscuits on top. Cover with the slices of
cheese and bake at 350 degrees for 25 - 30 minutes.

CHEESEBURGER AND CREAM CHEESE CASSEROLE

1 1/2 lb. hamburger
1 med. onion
8 oz pkg. cream cheese
4 oz shredded cheddar cheese
1/2 c. milk
1/3 c. catsup
1 can biscuits
1 can cream of mushroom soup

Brown onion and hamburger. Combine cream cheese and cheddar cheese, soup, milk, and catsup in casserole. Stir in hamburger and onion. Cover and bake at 350 degrees for 15 minutes. Remove cover and place biscuits on top, bake at 425 degrees until brown.

"SNOWBIRD'S" WHITE CHILI

1 lb. cooked chicken breasts skinned and chopped
1 large jar White Northern Beans- rinsed
1 jar salsa (8 – 12 oz.)
8 oz. pkg. Monterey Jack Cheese - cubed
2 tsp. cumin

Put all ingredients in a crock pot and let stew for several hours.

"AT-THE-TURN" BREAKFAST SOUFFLE

**2 lb. sausage – crumbled
9 eggs – slightly beaten
3 c. milk
1/2 tsp. dry mustard
1 tsp. salt
3 slices bread crumbs
1 1/2 c. grated cheddar cheese**

Brown sausage and drain. Mix remaining ingredients. Stir in sausage. Pour into 9 x 13 greased pan. Cover and refrigerate over night. Bake uncovered at 350 degrees for 1 hour.

"NEW MEXICO" CHICKEN ENCHIBENNI

1 large can evaporated milk
1 can cream of mushroom soup
2 cans cheddar cheese soup
1/2 c. onion – chopped
chili powder to taste
4 oz. can diced green chili's
1 whole cooked chicken - deboned and chopped
tortilla chips

Place above together (except tortilla chips) in saucepan and cook over low heat until thoroughly mixed. In casserole dish, place a layer of tortilla chips, then a layer of cream mixture. Alternate until used up. Bake at 350 degrees for 30 minutes.

"THE PRO'S" EGG, CHEESE, POTATO BUSINESS
(This is really good.)

24 oz. pkg. potatoes O'Brien hash browns
1 doz. eggs
1 lb. Mexican Velveeta Cheese

1. In large frying pan, using margarine, cook frozen hash browns over medium to high heat until cooked and browned. Set aside in bowl.

2. Scramble one dozen eggs and set aside in separate bowl.

3. Place cooked hash browns back into frying pan, and sprinkle scrambled eggs over the top. Over low heat, cover with cheese cut into slices. Cover until cheese begins to melt. Remove from heat and serve. Top with salsa if desired.

- **Mental Preparations Before the Swing:** The best mental preparation is to visualize in your mind the shot you want to play.
- Visualization lets you see the flight of the ball, how and where the ball lands, and the final results.

Soups,
Salads
&
Sauces

"SEVEN – UP" SALAD

1 c. hot water
1 small pkg. lemon jello
1 tsp. sugar
1 1/2 tsp. vanilla flavoring
8 oz. crushed pineapple
1/2 c. chopped red cherries
8 oz. cream cheese
8 oz. 7-Up soda
3/4 c. chopped pecans

Chill: lemon jello, hot water, and sugar.
Add remaining ingredients and stir. Chill for 5 - 7 hours
before serving.

"FIVE MAN SCRAMBLE" SALAD

1 can mandarin oranges
1 c. miniature marshmallows
1 lg. can chunky pineapple
1 c. coconut
1 c. sour cream

Drain all juice from fruit and mix well in sour cream. Chill
well before serving.

"BERMUDA GREEN" PISTACHIO SALAD

1 lg. can crushed pineapple
1 pkg. instant pistachio pudding
9 oz pkg. cool whip
1 c. small marshmallows
1/2 c. nuts – chopped

Place pineapple in mixing bowl. Sprinkle pudding over pineapple and leave for about 10 minutes. Then mix cool whip, nuts and marshmallows and fold into pineapple mixture. Refrigerate before serving.

Topping the Ball:
- **Causes:** The ball may be too far ahead in your stance, weight stays on the backside, target arm may be bending, or you may be taking your eyes off the ball.
- **Cures:** Move the ball in your stance, transfer your weight back to the target side, keep target arm straight, and keep your mind and eyes focused on the ball.

"SCRAMBLE" JELLO SALAD

1 pkg. lemon or line gelatin
1 c. water
1 tbsp. vinegar
1/2 c. mayonnaise
1 c. carrots – shredded
1 c. celery – chopped
1 tbsp. onions
1/2 lb. cottage cheese
1/2 c. non-dairy whipped topping
1 c. pineapple - chopped or diced

Mix and soft-set first 3 ingredients. Add remaining ingredients and stir until mixed thoroughly. Refrigerate.

"4-BALL" SALAD

4 c. boiling water
4 c. ice cream
4 small pkgs. gelatin (any 4 flavors)
12 oz. sour cream

Mix I c. boiling water, I c. ice cream and I pkg. gelatin together. Pour into 8 x 11 pan and chill until set. Add a thin layer of sour cream. Repeat process for each color, chilling between each layer.

"UNDULATING GREENS" SALAD

1 head of lettuce – torn
4 stalks of celery – chopped
1 onion – chopped
1 green pepper – chopped
1 pkg. frozen peas (small box)
2 c. mayonnaise
2 tbsp. sugar
8 oz. Swiss cheese – shredded
1/2 jar imitation bacon bits

Line bottom of shallow pan with lettuce; layer the remaining ingredients in order listed. DO NOT TOSS OR STIR. Refrigerate several hours or overnight.

- Breaking Putts: If you feel the ball will break 6 inches, then aim for and align your stance 6 inches and look at the spot where you want the ball to roll.
- Remember that you are putting to a spot and not a hole on breaking putts.

"DOGLEG" CHICKEN BOWL

8 oz. can kidney beans – drained
8 oz. cooked chicken – cut into strips
3 oz. cheddar cheese – cut into strips
1/3 cucumber – sliced
1/2 c. celery – sliced
1/4 c. vinegar
3 tbsp. sugar
1 tsp. grated onion
1/4 tsp. salt
1/4 tsp. celery seed
1/4 tsp. dry mustard
1/8 tsp. paprika
1/2 c. salad oil
5 c. torn lettuce and or/spinach
1 large tomato – cut into wedges

Combine beans, chicken, cheese, cucumber and celery; chill. Mix vinegar, sugar, onion, salt, celery seed, mustard and paprika. Slowly add salad oil, stirring constantly. Chill dressing. Toss lettuce with bean and chicken mix and add dressing. Garnish with tomato wedges.

CURRIED NUT-AND-FRUIT SALAD

1 head red leaf or romaine lettuce
1 c. torn spinach
1 c. grapes halved and seeded
1 (11 oz.) can mandarin oranges – chilled and drained

DRESSING:
1/2 c. salad oil
1/3 c. wine vinegar
2 garlic cloves – minced
2 tbsp. brown sugar
1 tbsp. curry powder
1 tsp. soy sauce
1 avocado – peeled and sliced
1/4 c. toasted slivered almonds

Toss lettuce, spinach, grapes, and mandarin oranges together. In covered container or jar combine oil, vinegar, garlic, brown sugar, curry powder, and soy sauce. Pour a small amount over salad to coat. Serve the remaining amount as dressing. Top with almonds and sliced avocado.

"BIRDIE" FRUIT SALAD

7 c. torn spinach leaves
1 c. celery – sliced
8 oz. can pineapple chunks with juice
2 apples – cored and wedged
1 orange – peeled and sectioned
3/4 lb. chicken or turkey - cut into strips

Toss spinach and celery in a salad bowl. Drain pineapple and save juice. Dip apple wedges in juice from pineapple. Spread orange slices, chicken, pineapple and apple wedges on top of spinach. Top with your favorite dressing.

BROCCOLI-CAULIFLOWER-RAISIN SALAD

1 c. mayonnaise
1/3 c. sugar
3 tbsp. vinegar
1 med. cauliflower cut into bite size
1/4 c. chopped onions
4 c. chopped broccoli
1/2 c. raisins
8 slices cooked bacon – crisp and crumbled

Combine first 3 ingredients; add next 5 ingredients to mayonnaise mixture. Cool 2 hours before serving.

HOT ALMOND-CURRIED FRUIT SALAD

1 can (29 oz) can sliced peaches – drained
1 can (15 oz) pineapple chunks – drained
1 can (16 oz) pear halves – drained
1 jar maraschino cherries – drained
1/3 c. slivered almonds
1/3 c. margarine – melted
3/4 c. brown sugar
1 tbsp. curry powder

Place first 4 ingredients in a 9 x 13 baking dish and sprinkle with almonds. Combine margarine, brown sugar and curry powder. Top fruit with brown sugar mixture and bake a 325 degrees for 1 hour.

CREAMY POTATO SOUP

1/4 c. margarine
1 c. chopped onion
2 stalks celery – chopped
1/4 c. flour
4 c. cubed potatoes
6 – 8 oz. mushrooms – chopped/sliced (optional)
3 c. milk
1 c. half & half
2 tsp. salt

Melt margarine in large saucepan or Dutch oven. Add onion and celery and sauté until tender, about 15 minutes. Blend in flour. Add milk, half & half, potatoes and salt, stirring frequently. Cover and simmer about 45 minutes. Add mushrooms and simmer until mushrooms and potatoes are tender. Serve hot, sprinkled with bacon bits and parmesan cheese.

- Golf Swing Mental Image:
- Think of your body in a large barrel with you rotating inside of it. You can't sway back and forth or up and down.
- How you are at the address position is how you should be when you hit the ball.

POTATO SALAD

4 med. potatoes – peeled and cubed
1 bay leaf
several celery leaves
1 c. celery – chopped
1/3 c. green pepper – chopped
1/3 c. onion – chopped
3 hard-boiled eggs – chopped
2 tbsp. snipped parsley
1 c. mayonnaise
1 tsp. prepared mustard

In saucepan, place first 3 ingredients, cover with water and 1 tsp. salt. Boil covered until tender then drain. Combine potatoes, celery, and next 4 ingredients. Mix mayonnaise, salt, and mustard and toss with potato mixture. Cover and chill. Serves 6 – 8.

MOM'S HOMEMADE 1000 ISLAND DRESSING

1 c. salad dressing
catsup to color
1 tbsp. onion – chopped
1 tbsp. sweet relish
3 eggs boiled and chopped fine

In bowl mix ingredients together, and add more of what you like to create your own taste. Chill before serving.

HOT FUDGE SAUCE

3 squares of unsweetened chocolate
2 tbsp. margarine
1 c. sugar
1 large can evaporated milk

Melt chocolate and add margarine. Stir in sugar and gradually add evaporated milk. Stir 20 – 30 minutes over medium heat until thick.

- The Chip Shot: Weight on the target side, knees flexed, hands in front of the ball at address.
- With feet together, hands, arms and shoulders swing as one unit.

HOT DOG SAUCE

3/4 c. beer
1 1/2 c. catsup
1/2 c. brown sugar
1 tbsp. minced onion
2 pkgs. hot dogs – cooked & cut into 1" pieces

Mix first 4 ingredients and bring to a boil; reduce heat and simmer for 10 minutes. Serve over cooked hot dogs.

SAUCES FOR HAM

PINEAPPLE SAUCE:

1 can crushed pineapple, plus juice
1 c. orange juice
1/2 c. sugar
cornstarch and water to thicken

Heat and stir in sauce pan until thick. Serve over ham or on the side.

RAISIN SAUCE

1/2 c. brown sugar
2 tbsp. flour
1/2 tsp. mustard
4 tbsp. vinegar
1/2 c. raisins
1 1/2 c. hot water

Combine all ingredients and cook slowly until slightly thickened and well blended. Serve over ham or on the side.

THE
19TH
HOLE

"RAINY WEATHER" FIRESIDE COFFEE

2 c. hot chocolate mix
2 c. coffee creamer
1 c. instant coffee
1 1/2 c. sugar
1 tsp. cinnamon
1/2 tsp. nutmeg

Mix thoroughly and add 3 - 4 tsp. to 1 c. hot water.

Rainy and Wet Weather:
- What is there to say but KEEP DRY, not only you but your equipment as well. Plus, water will accumulate on the ball causing it to travel less, so use more club.

"INTERNATIONAL" SPICED TEA

1 1/2 c. fine grained instant tea
18 oz. jar Tang
5 oz. pkg. presweetened lemonade
1/2 tsp. allspice
3/4 tsp. ground cloves
1 tsp. cinnamon
10 oz. pkg. red hots

Mix thoroughly and add 2 heaping tsp. to 1 cup hot water.

"NINE – DEGREE LOFT" PUNCH

1 large can pineapple juice
3 cans frozen orange juice
3 cans frozen lemonade
6 c. brewed tea
6 c. sugar
8 quarts gingerale

Dissolve sugar in 6 c. water and add brewed tea.
Combine and add juices plus water per directions on
frozen juice cans. Freeze, stirring several times. Last
stirring use electric mixer. When serving add gingerale
as needed to make it liquid.

HOT APPLE CIDER

2 bottles apple cider
1 bottle cranberry juice
1 tbsp. allspice
1/2 c. brown sugar
4 cinnamon sticks
1 orange
2 – 4 whole cloves

In large pan add above ingredients. Cut orange in
slices before adding (peel and all). Heat on low for
3 – 4 hours.

CRANBERRY PUNCH

4 c. cranberry juice
4 c. pineapple juice
2 c. apple or orange juice
1 1/2 c. sugar
1 Tbsp. almond extract
2 qt. gingerale

Mix all juices with sugar until dissolved. Add extract.
Chill and add gingerale just before serving.

ORANGE – PEACH COOLER

1 medium peach – peeled and sliced
1 c. orange juice
1/4 c. dry milk powder
8 ice cubes

In blender combine all ingredients. Cover and blend
until smooth. Serves 2.

"AFTER-A-ROUND" VODKA LEMON SLUSH

9 c. water
2 c. sugar
4 tea bags
1 fifth vodka (or whiskey)
12 oz. can frozen orange juice concentrate – thawed
12 oz. can frozen lemonade concentrate – thawed

Boil water and sugar until sugar is dissolved. Remove from heat and add tea bags. Cool to room temperature. Add vodka, orange juice, and lemonade. Mix well and freeze for 8 – 12 hours. Remove, stir and refreeze. Keep frozen.

To mix: fill glass about 3/4 full and add 7-UP, Sprite, or Gingerale. Stir and enjoy!

CHRISTMAS EGGNOG

8 eggs
1 fifth bourbon
4 qt. whole milk
1 c. superfine sugar
salt to taste
1/2 tsp. nutmeg - grated
1/2 pint whipped cream

Separate 8 eggs. Beat yolks and slowly add bourbon.
Beat. Add milk and beat again. Add sugar through the
mixer beaters. Beat egg whites and sweeten to taste,
then beat into eggnog. Beat again with nutmeg. Add
salt to taste. Fold in 1/2 pint whipped cream,
sweetened to taste. Dollop with whipped cream to
taste. Decorate with grated nutmeg.

Let stand 1 – 2 days before drinking. Makes 5 – 6 quarts.
Happy Holidays!

"PENALTY STROKE" CRANBERRY WINE COOLER

32 oz. bottle cranberry juice cocktail – chilled
12 oz. can lemon-lime soda – chilled
3/4 c. dry red wine – chilled
whole fresh strawberries

In 2-qt. pitcher stir together chilled beverages. Pour over ice-filled glasses and garnish with fresh strawberries.

- Penalty Strokes: Just a couple of reminders:
- Don't ground your club in a water hazard, or bunker.
- If you are cleaning around the ball on the fairway and the ball moves before you swing, it's considered a stroke so don't forget to count it.

JUNIOR GOLF

MUNCHIES

"COCA-COLA" SALAD

12 oz can of coke
4 oz. cream cheese
1 small can crushed pineapple
1 pkg. cherry jello
1 c. boiling pineapple juice
1 c. chopped mixed nuts

Mix everything together and chill 8 hours.
*Kids will love it

- Reading Greens: Remember that putts break toward water and away from mountains.
- Also, if the greens are moist or wet, they will be slower and break less than you think.

"SCORERS TABLE" CRACKER SNAX

1 pkg. original ranch dressing mix
1 c. oil
1/2 tsp. lemon pepper (more if desired)
2 tsp. dill weed (more if desired)
1 tsp. garlic salt
2 pkg. oyster crackers

Mix first 5 ingredients in large bowl. Add crackers and toss. Keep in airtight containers.

"JUNIOR GOLF CHAMPION" – SLOPPY JOE PIZZA

1 lb. ground beef
3/4 c. frozen corn – defrosted
3/4 c. barbecue sauce
1/2 c. green onions – chopped
1/2 tsp. salt
1 large Italian bread or pizza crust
1 1/2 c. shredded cheese

Brown ground beef and pour off grease. Stir in corn, barbecue sauce, onions and salt. Heat through. With pizza shell on baking sheet; spoon beef mixture over top and sprinkle with cheese. Bake at 425 degrees for 12 - 15 minutes or until cheese is melted.

- **The Sand Shot: The major goal in all sand shots is to GET OUT!**
- **Check the sand. Soft or fine sand will require swinging a little harder and fuller.**
- **For wet sand try to cut your swing down as the ball will have a tendency to fly farther.**

"TIN CUPS"

1 c. peanut butter
1 box confectioners sugar
1 stick margarine – softened
1 pkg. microwaveable chocolate squares

Mix first 3 ingredients well, and shape into balls.
Refrigerate. Melt chocolate squares. Dip balls in
chocolate and place on wax paper. Keep in cool
place.

COOKIES – QUICK AND EASY

1 cake mix (any flavor)
2 eggs
1/2 c. oil
***

Mix above. Spoon onto nonstick cookie sheet and
bake at 350 degrees for 10 minutes.

***Add any of the following for fun:
nuts
chocolate chips
M&M's

"STICKY-FINGER" CINNAMON CRESCENT ROLLS

2 pkgs. crescent rolls
Mix:
1/4 c. sugar
2 tsp. cinnamon

1/4 c. margarine - melted
1 pkg. large marshmallows

Dip marshmallows (one per crescent roll) in margarine and then in sugar and cinnamon mixture. Put on wide end of crescent roll and roll up. Pinch edges together. Dip in margarine and sugar mixture again. Bake on greased muffin tins as directed on crescent roll wrapper. Note there are usually 8 rolls to a package.

CHOCOLATE MALT FROZEN DESSERT

Crust:
1/3 c. soft margarine
1 1/2 c. graham cracker crumbs
Mix and pat in bottom of 8 x 11 pan.

Filling:
2 c. chocolate ice cream softened
1 tbsp. milk
2 c. malted milk balls - crushed
Mix and spread on top of crust.

Topping:
8 oz. non-dairy whipped topping
3 Tbsp. malt powder
1 c. malted milk balls – crushed

Mix and layer whipped topping and powder on top of filling. Sprinkle with crushed malted milk balls. Freeze and serve.

"CHIPS AND PUTTS"

1 box rice chex
1 box corn chex
1 box wheat chex
1 box cherrios
1 bag pretzel sticks
1 can honey roasted nuts
1 can mixed nuts

Mix together and set aside.

Sauce mix:
3 sticks margarine
4 Tbsp. Worcestershire sauce
4 tsp. garlic salt
2 tsp. onion salt
3 tsp. celery salt

In a saucepan melt margarine, then add sauce mix ingredients and stir. Heat oven to 250 degrees. Pour sauce over cereal, nut, and pretzel mixture in large shallow pan. Bake 45 minutes at 250 degrees stirring every 15 minutes.

"THE TEE BOX" NIBBLE MIX

4-6 c. popped popcorn (any flavor)
2 c. cheerios
2 c. bite-sized shredded wheat squares
1 c. mixed nuts
1/2 c. raisins (optional)
3 tbsp. butter or margarine, melted
1/3 c. grated Parmesan cheese
1 1/2 tbsp. dry Italian salad dressing mix

In 13 x 9 x 2 (or larger) inch baking pan combine popcorn, cheerios, wheat squares, and nuts. Heat in 300 degree oven for about 5 minutes. Remove and add raisins. Sprinkle with butter. Combine cheese and salad dressing mix, sprinkle over mixture and stir. Makes about 9 - 11 cups.

"SLICE & HOOK " FRUIT PIZZA

1 roll sugar cookie dough
8 oz. cream cheese
8 oz. cool whip
bananas
grapes
apples
kiwi fruit
strawberry's
any type fruit you like

Press cookie dough flat and spread with oil. Bake at 325 degrees for 10 minutes or until golden brown. Let cool. Blend cream cheese and cool whip and spread on top of cookie dough. Slice your favorite fruits and decorate.

**Optional – Glaze for topping

1 c. orange juice
2 tbsp. corn starch
1 tsp. lemon juice
sweeten with sugar to desired taste

Boil till thick, cool before pouring on fruit.

"GRAPHITE SHAFT" SAND DABS

1 stick margarine – very soft
4 heaping tbsp. powdered sugar
2 c. flour
1/2 tbsp. ice water
2 tsp. vanilla
1 c. nuts – chopped

Cream sugar and margarine. Mix other ingredients and work into margarine and sugar mixture. Pinch off small pieces and shape into size of small finger. Bake in 250 degree oven for 30 - 40 minutes. Roll in powered sugar when cool.

- **Ball Above Your Feet: Choke down on the grip.**
- **This position will cause your swing to be flatter which will cause the ball to fly to the left.**
- **Aim to the right to compensate for the hook.**
- **And keep your weight on the balls of your feet.**

About the Author:

Born and raised in Michigan, Christi began her golfing career in 1978, and became a member of the LPGA in 1980. Since then she has been teaching and playing golf with her students, friends, and family. Still teaching occasionally, her interests are now in running her new business, "The Classic Difference", playing more golf, cooking and traveling.